KS1
5–7
Years

Master Maths at Home

Fractions

Scan the QR code to help
your child's learning at home.

 | **MATHS**
NO PROBLEM! ◻

mastermathsathome.com

How to use this book

Maths — No Problem! created **Master Maths at Home** to help children develop fluency in the subject and a rich understanding of core concepts.

Key features of the Master Maths at Home books include:

- Carefully designed lessons that provide structure but also allow flexibility in how they're used. For example, some children may want to write numbers, while others might want to trace.

- Speech bubbles containing content designed to spark diverse conversations, with many discussion points that don't have obvious 'right' or 'wrong' answers.

- Rich illustrations that will guide children to a discussion of shapes and units of measurement, allowing them to make connections to the wider world around them.

- Exercises that allow a flexible approach and can be adapted to suit any child's cognitive or functional ability.

- Clearly laid out pages that encourage children to practise a range of higher-order skills.

- A community of friendly and relatable characters who introduce each lesson and come along as your child progresses through the series.

You can see more guidance on how to use these books at **mastermathsathome.com**.

We're excited to share all the ways you can learn maths!

Maths — No Problem!
mastermathsathome.com
www.mathsnoproblem.com
hello@mathsnoproblem.com

First published in Great Britain in 2022 by
Dorling Kindersley Limited
One Embassy Gardens, 8 Viaduct Gardens, London SW11 7BW
A Penguin Random House Company

The authorised representative in the EEA is Dorling Kindersley
Verlag GmbH. Amulfstr. 124, 80636 Munich, Germany

10 9 8 7 6 5 4 3 2 1
001–327070–Jan/22

This book was made with Forest Stewardship Council™ certified paper – one small step in DK's commitment to a sustainable future. For more information go to www.dk.com/our-green-pledge

A CIP catalogue record for this book is available from the British Library.

ISBN: 978-0-24153-912-5
Printed and bound in China

For the curious
www.dk.com

Acknowledgements
The publisher would like to thank the authors and consultants Andy Psarianos, Judy Hornigold, Adam Gifford and Dr Anne Hermanson.

The Castledown typeface has been used with permission from the Colophon Foundry.

Contents

Ruby   Elliott   Amira   Charles   Lulu   Sam   Oak   Holly   Ravi   Emma   Jacob   Hannah

Equal parts

Starter

Four friends want to share a pizza so everyone gets the same amount.
Ruby cuts the square pizza this way.

I think all these pieces are the same amount. All 4 pieces are equal.

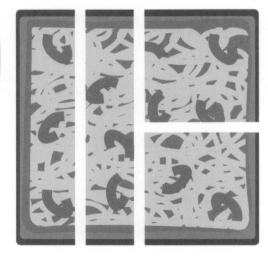

The pieces are different shapes. I don't think they are the same size.

Who is correct?

Example

First I cut the pizza in 2 equal parts like this.

step 1

I then cut one of the pieces into 2 smaller equal pieces.

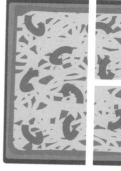

step 2

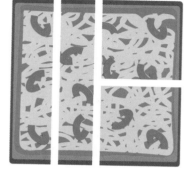

step 3

Then I cut the other piece into 2 smaller equal pieces in another way.

I think 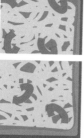 is correct. The pieces don't look the same but they are the same size.

If all the pieces are the same size, we can say the 4 pieces are equal.

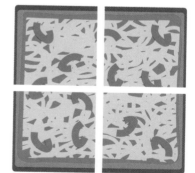  

These are some other ways that Ruby could have cut the pizza.

Are all these pieces equal?

5

1 Draw lines to cut each shape into 2 equal parts.
Try to find more than 1 way.

(a)

(b)

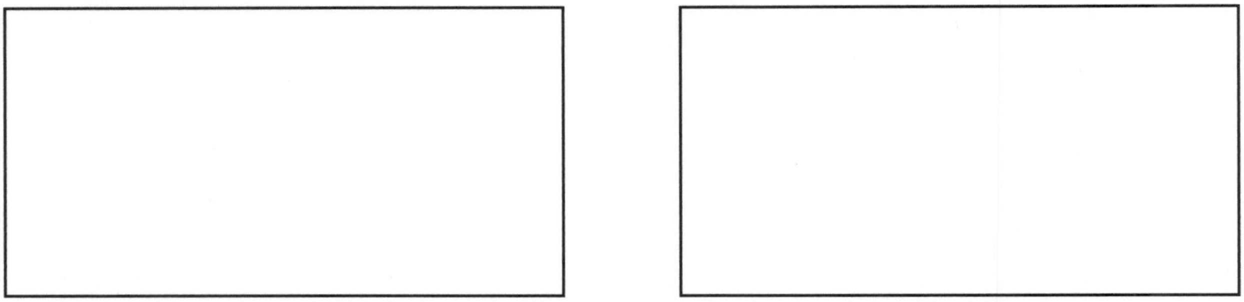

2 Draw lines to cut each shape into 4 equal parts.
Try to find more than 1 way.

(a)

(b)

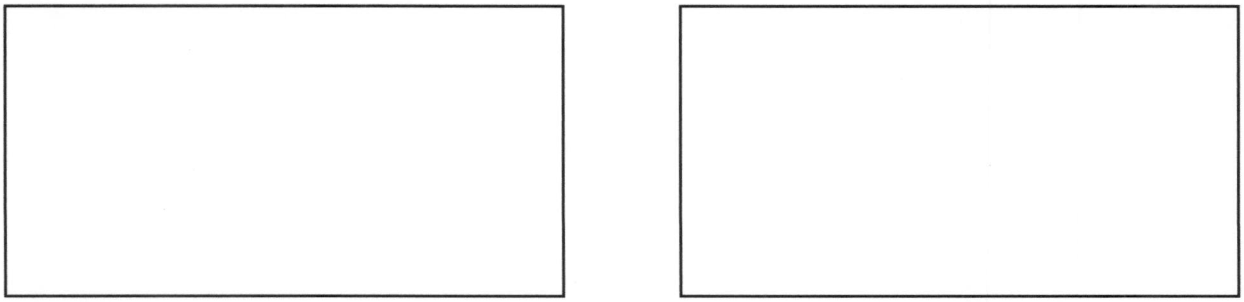

3 Circle the shapes that show equal parts.

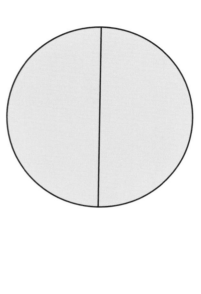

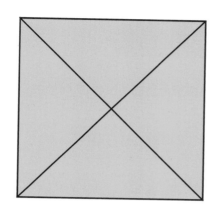

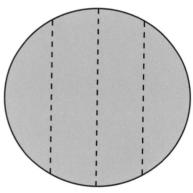

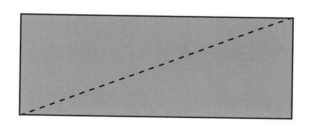

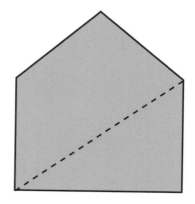

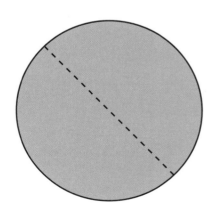

Halves and quarters

Starter

Can you help Elliott fold a piece of paper into 2 equal parts?

What about folding the piece of paper into 4 equal parts?

Example

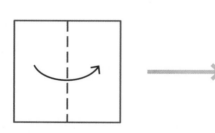  

Fold the square piece of paper to show 2 equal parts.

There are 2 equal parts.
Each piece is 1 half of the whole paper.
Each piece is 1 part out of 2 equal parts.

We can write this as $\frac{1}{2}$.

We say **one half**.

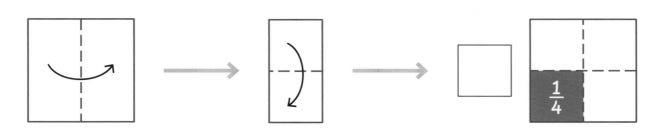

There are 4 equal parts.
Each piece is 1 quarter of the whole paper.
Each piece is 1 part out of 4 equal parts.

We can write this as $\frac{1}{4}$.

We say **one quarter**.

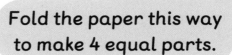

Fold the paper this way to make 4 equal parts.

Practice

Match the pictures that show $\frac{1}{2}$ and $\frac{1}{4}$.

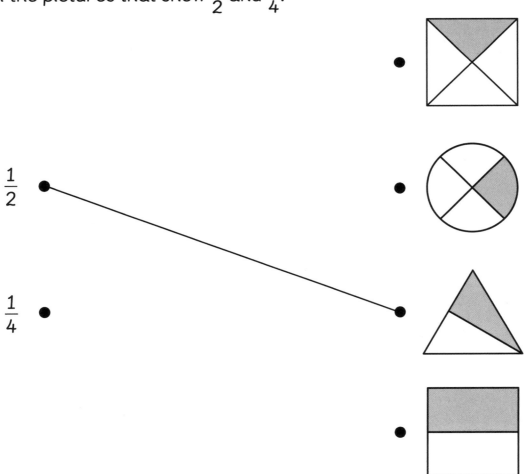

Thirds

Starter

2 parts of the strip of paper are shaded.

How much of the paper is not shaded?

Example

The strip of paper is divided into 3 equal parts. Each piece is called a **third**.

$\frac{1}{3}$	$\frac{1}{3}$	$\frac{1}{3}$

1 third = $\frac{1}{3}$

2 thirds = $\frac{2}{3}$

2 thirds of the paper is shaded.
1 third of the paper is not shaded.

$\frac{1}{3}$ of the paper is not shaded.

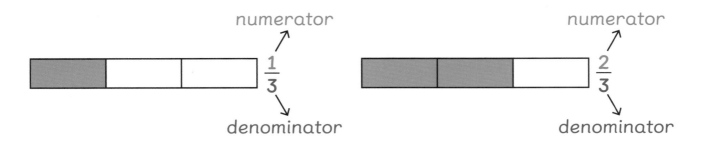

The **numerator** tells us the number of parts.

The **denominator** tells us the number of equal parts the item is divided into.

Practice

What fraction of each shape is shaded?

1

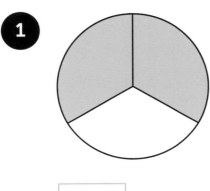

$\frac{\boxed{}}{3}$ $\boxed{}$ thirds

2

$\frac{\boxed{}}{3}$ $\boxed{}$ third

3

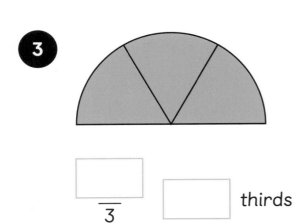

$\frac{\boxed{}}{3}$ $\boxed{}$ thirds

Recognise, name and write fractions

Starter

How much of each strip is shaded?

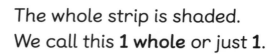

Example

1

The whole strip is shaded.
We call this **1 whole** or just **1**.

$\frac{1}{2}$	$\frac{1}{2}$

The strip is in two equal parts.
We call these parts **halves**.
1 half is shaded.
We write 1 half like this $\frac{1}{2}$.

> When we cut 1 whole into parts, we can name the parts. The parts must be equal before we can name them.

$\frac{1}{3}$	$\frac{1}{3}$	$\frac{1}{3}$

The strip is in three equal parts.
We call these parts **thirds**.
2 thirds are shaded.
We write 2 thirds like this $\frac{2}{3}$.

$\frac{1}{4}$	$\frac{1}{4}$	$\frac{1}{4}$	$\frac{1}{4}$

The strip is in four equal parts.
We call these parts **quarters**.
3 quarters are shaded.
We write 3 quarters like this $\frac{3}{4}$.

> $\frac{3}{4}$
> The numerator is 3.
> The denominator is 4.

1 What fraction of each shape is shaded?

(a)

[ ] out of [ ] parts are shaded.

[ ] is the numerator.

[ ] is the denominator.

(b)

[ ] out of [ ] parts is shaded.

[ ] is the numerator.

[ ] is the denominator.

(c)

[ ] out of [ ] parts is shaded.

[ ] is the numerator.

[ ] is the denominator.

2 What fraction of the shape is shaded?
What fraction of the shape is not shaded?

shaded

[ ]
──
[ ]

not shaded

[ ]
──
[ ]

Equal fractions

Starter

I ate 1 piece of my tart.

I ate 2 pieces of my tart.

Did they eat the same amount of tart?

14

I cut my tart into 2 equal pieces. Each piece is $\frac{1}{2}$ of the whole tart. I ate 1 of these pieces.

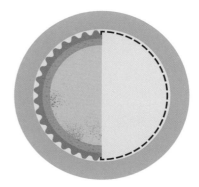

I cut my tart into 4 equal pieces. Each piece is $\frac{1}{4}$ of the whole tart. I ate 2 of these pieces.

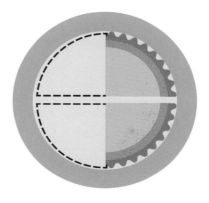

 and ate the same amount of tart.

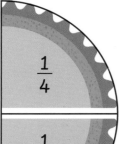

$\frac{1}{4}$

$\frac{1}{4}$

$\frac{1}{2}$

$\frac{2}{4}$ = $\frac{1}{2}$

2 quarters of the tart is the same as 1 half of the tart.

1 Match the fractions to make 1 whole.

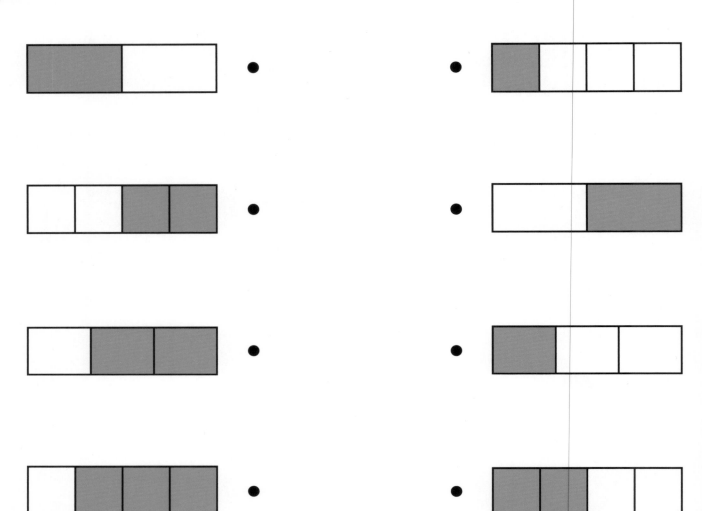

2 Use the chart to help you fill in the blanks.

1

| $\frac{1}{2}$ | $\frac{1}{2}$ |

| $\frac{1}{3}$ | $\frac{1}{3}$ | $\frac{1}{3}$ |

| $\frac{1}{4}$ | $\frac{1}{4}$ | $\frac{1}{4}$ | $\frac{1}{4}$ |

(a) $\dfrac{\boxed{}}{2} = 1$

(b) $\dfrac{\boxed{}}{3} = 1$

(c) $\dfrac{3}{\boxed{}} = 1$

(d) $\dfrac{\boxed{}}{4} = 1$

(e) $\dfrac{1}{\boxed{}} = \dfrac{2}{4}$

(f) $\dfrac{\boxed{}}{4} = \dfrac{1}{2}$

Comparing like fractions

Starter

Charles and Ruby both cut their pizzas into 4 equal-sized pieces.

Ruby eats 2 slices and Charles eats 1 slice.

Who eats more pizza?

Example

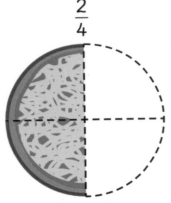

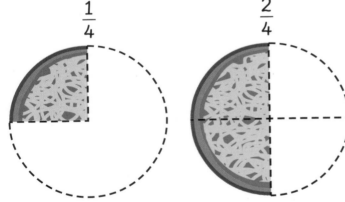

$$\frac{2}{4} > \frac{1}{4}$$

Ruby eats more pizza than Charles.

A piece of pizza is called a **slice**.

$\frac{2}{4}$ is greater than $\frac{1}{4}$. We use > to mean **greater than** and < to mean **less than**.

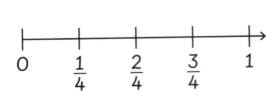

We can show fractions on a number line as well.

Practice

1 Shade and fill in the blanks.

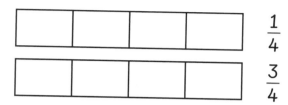

$\frac{1}{4}$

$\frac{3}{4}$

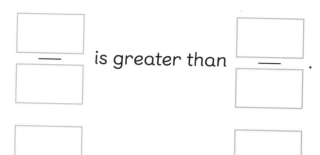

_____ is greater than _____.

_____ is smaller than _____.

2 Arrange the fractions in order.

(a) Start with the greatest.

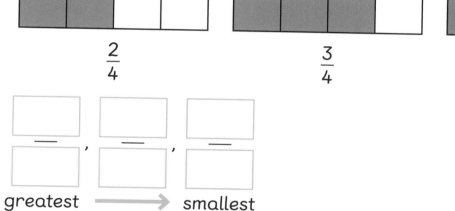

$\frac{2}{4}$

$\frac{3}{4}$

$\frac{1}{4}$

_____ , _____ , _____

greatest ⟶ smallest

(b) Start with the smallest.

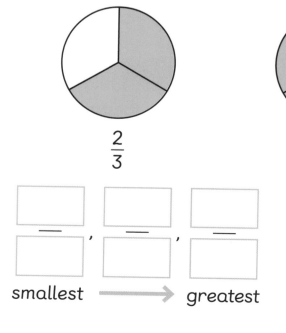

$\frac{2}{3}$

$\frac{3}{3}$

$\frac{1}{3}$

_____ , _____ , _____

smallest ⟶ greatest

Comparing unlike fractions

Starter

I think $\frac{1}{3}$ is more than $\frac{1}{2}$.

I don't agree. I think $\frac{1}{2}$ is more than $\frac{1}{3}$.

Who is correct?

Example

I can draw number lines to check.

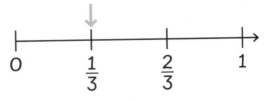

| 0 | | $\frac{1}{3}$ | | $\frac{2}{3}$ | | 1 | |

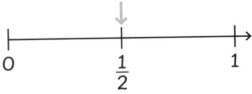

| 0 | | $\frac{1}{2}$ | | 1 |

I like to use paper strips.

$\frac{1}{2}$	$\frac{1}{2}$

$\frac{1}{3}$	$\frac{1}{3}$	$\frac{1}{3}$

 is correct.

$\frac{1}{2} > \frac{1}{3}$

1 half is more than 1 third.

1 Fill in the blanks. Use > or <.

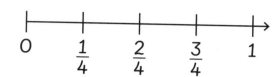

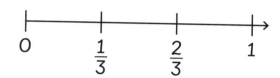

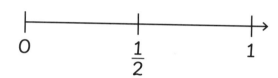

(a) $\frac{1}{4}$ ☐ $\frac{1}{2}$

(b) $\frac{1}{3}$ ☐ $\frac{1}{4}$

(c) $\frac{1}{3}$ ☐ $\frac{1}{2}$

2 Arrange the fractions in order.
Start with the smallest.

$\frac{1}{4}$

$\frac{1}{2}$

$\frac{1}{3}$

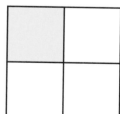

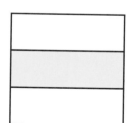

 , ,

smallest ➝ greatest

Whole numbers and fractions

Starter

Ravi and Emma want to share 3 muffins equally.
How much does each of them get?

Example

Each of them gets a whole muffin.

They also get $\frac{1}{2}$ of a muffin each.

They both get 1 whole muffin and 1 half of a muffin.

They both get $1\frac{1}{2}$ muffins.

Practice

Count the number of pieces and fill in the blanks.

This is one piece.

1

2

3

4

Counting in halves

Starter

Sam and his mum buy some watermelon for the school picnic. How much watermelon do they buy?

Example

This is a whole watermelon. They buy 2 of these.

This is 1 half of a watermelon. They buy one of these.

They buy $2\frac{1}{2}$ watermelons. We say two and a half watermelons.

$$
\begin{array}{c|c|c|c|c|c|c}
0 & \frac{1}{2} & 1 & 1\frac{1}{2} & 2 & 2\frac{1}{2} & 3
\end{array}
$$

We can show $2\frac{1}{2}$ on a number line like this.

Practice

1 How many pieces are there? Fill in the blanks.

(a)

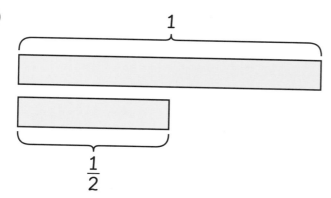

(b)

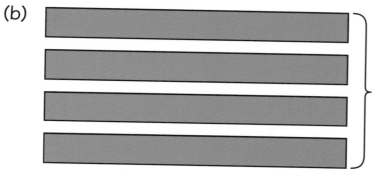

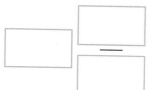

(c)

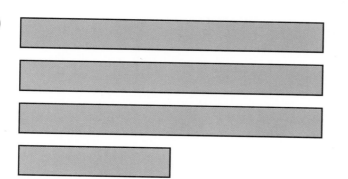

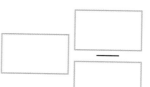

2 Fill in the blanks.

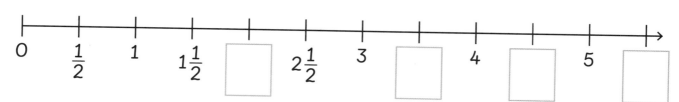

Counting in quarters

Starter

How much watermelon does the shopkeeper have left at the end of the day?

Example

This is 1 whole watermelon.

This is 1 quarter of a watermelon.

We can show $1\frac{1}{4}$ on a number line like this.

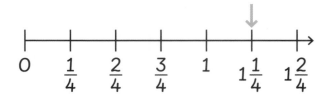

The shopkeeper has $1\frac{1}{4}$ watermelons left at the end of the day.

1 How many pieces are there? Fill in the blanks.

(a)

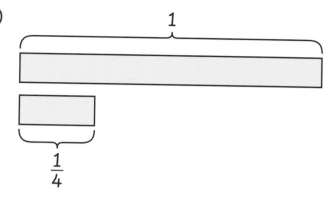

$\dfrac{1}{4}$

(b)

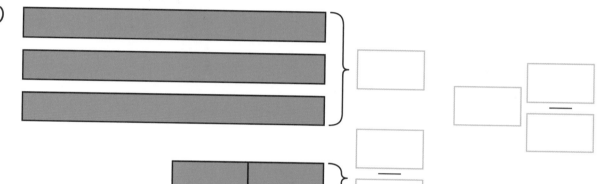

(c)

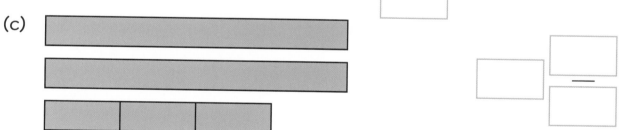

2 Fill in the blanks.

(a)

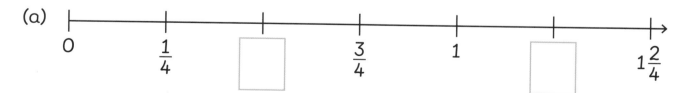

(b)

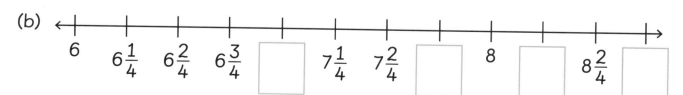

Counting in thirds

Starter

The pizza chef uses this many blocks of cheese to make pizzas.

How many blocks of cheese does the chef use?

Example

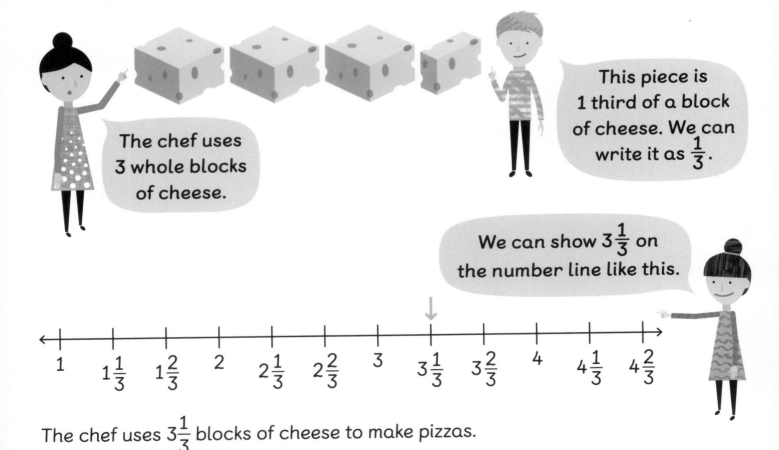

The chef uses 3 whole blocks of cheese.

This piece is 1 third of a block of cheese. We can write it as $\frac{1}{3}$.

We can show $3\frac{1}{3}$ on the number line like this.

| 1 | $1\frac{1}{3}$ | $1\frac{2}{3}$ | 2 | $2\frac{1}{3}$ | $2\frac{2}{3}$ | 3 | $3\frac{1}{3}$ | $3\frac{2}{3}$ | 4 | $4\frac{1}{3}$ | $4\frac{2}{3}$ |

The chef uses $3\frac{1}{3}$ blocks of cheese to make pizzas.

1 How many pieces are there? Fill in the blanks.

(a)

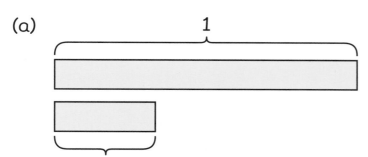

1

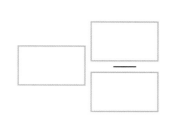

(b)

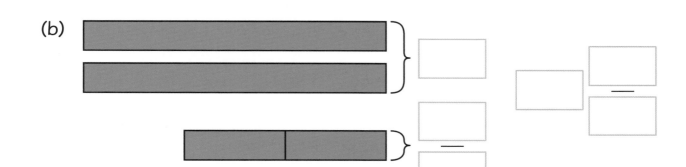

(c)

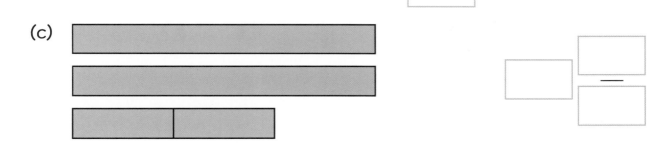

2 Fill in the blanks.

(a)

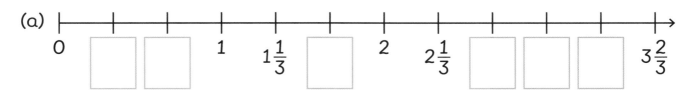

0 ☐ ☐ 1 $1\frac{1}{3}$ ☐ 2 $2\frac{1}{3}$ ☐ ☐ ☐ $3\frac{2}{3}$

(b)

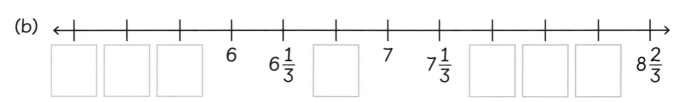

☐ ☐ ☐ 6 $6\frac{1}{3}$ ☐ 7 $7\frac{1}{3}$ ☐ ☐ ☐ $8\frac{2}{3}$

Half of a set

How many pieces does half of the chocolate bar have?

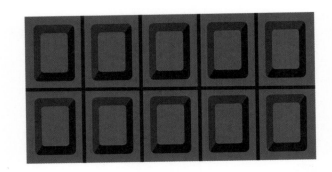

Example

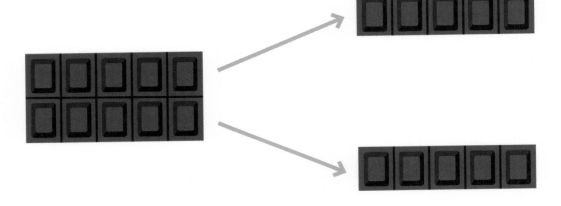

The whole chocolate bar has 10 pieces.

Half of the chocolate bar has half of the number of pieces.

Half of the chocolate bar has 5 pieces.

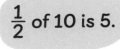

$\frac{1}{2}$ of 10 is 5.

Fill in the blanks.

1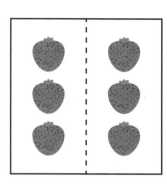

$\frac{1}{2}$ of 6 = ☐

2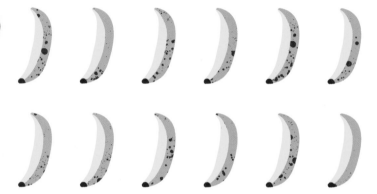

$\frac{1}{2}$ of 12 = ☐

3

$\frac{1}{2}$ of 4 = ☐

4

$\frac{1}{2}$ of 30 = ☐

Third of a set

Starter

The children each get $\frac{1}{3}$ of the strawberry cake.

How many strawberries will each of them get?

Example

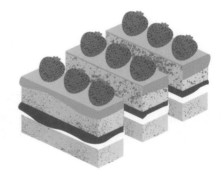

There are 9 strawberries on the whole cake. Each third has 3 strawberries.

$\frac{1}{3}$ of 9 is 3.

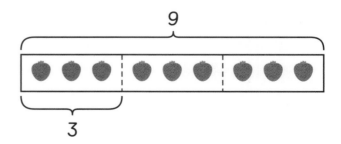

Each child will get 3 strawberries.

Fill in the blanks.

1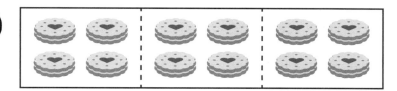

$\frac{1}{3}$ of 12 =

2

$\frac{1}{3}$ of 15 =

3

$\frac{1}{3}$ of 12 =

4

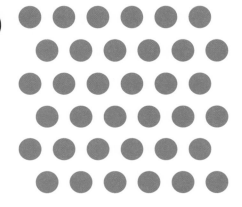

$\frac{1}{3}$ of 36 =

Quarter of a set

Starter

There are 36 counters in total. Each stack is $\frac{1}{4}$ of the total amount.

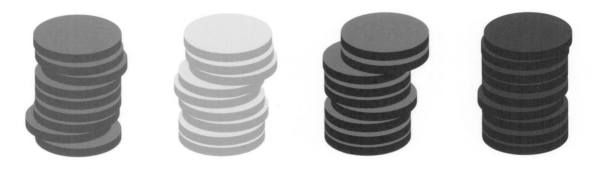

How many yellow counters are there?

Example

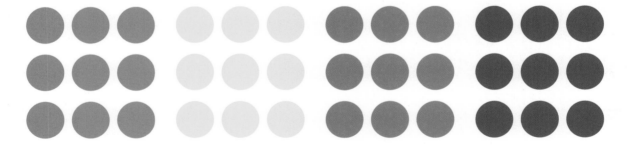

There are 36 counters in total.
1 quarter of the counters are yellow.

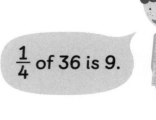

$\frac{1}{4}$ of 36 is 9.

There are 9 yellow counters.

Match.

$\frac{1}{4}$ of 12   ●

●   10

$\frac{1}{4}$ of 8   ●

●   2

$\frac{1}{4}$ of 4   ●

●   3

$\frac{1}{4}$ of 40   ●

●   8

$\frac{1}{4}$ of 32   ●

●   1

Fractions of a quantity

Starter

Amira's 3-year-old sister is half as tall as her dad. Her dad is 2 m tall.

How tall is Amira's sister?

Example

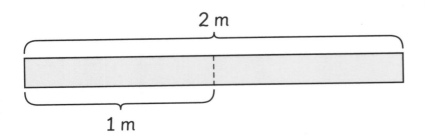

2 m

1 m

$\frac{1}{2}$ of 2 m = 1 m

Amira's dad is 2 m tall.
One half of 2 m is 1 m.

Fill in the blanks to solve the word problems.

1 The length of a car is $\frac{1}{4}$ of the length of a lorry. The lorry is 16 m. How long is the car?

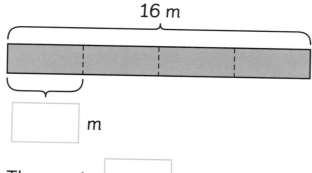

16 m

◻ m

$\frac{1}{4}$ of 16 m = ◻ m

The car is ◻ m long.

2 Jacob went shopping with his dad. They bought a jacket, a pair of trousers and a T-shirt.

(a) The jacket cost £48 and the trousers cost half of the price of the jacket. How much did the trousers cost?

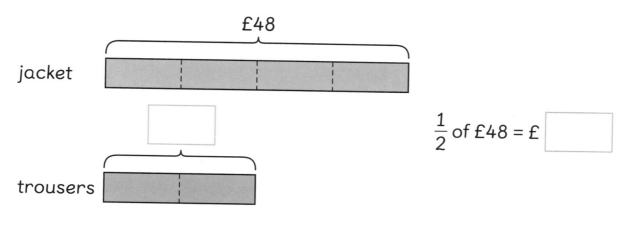

£48

jacket

trousers

$\frac{1}{2}$ of £48 = £ ◻

The trousers cost £ ◻ .

(b) The T-shirt cost half as much as the trousers. How much did the
     T-shirt cost?

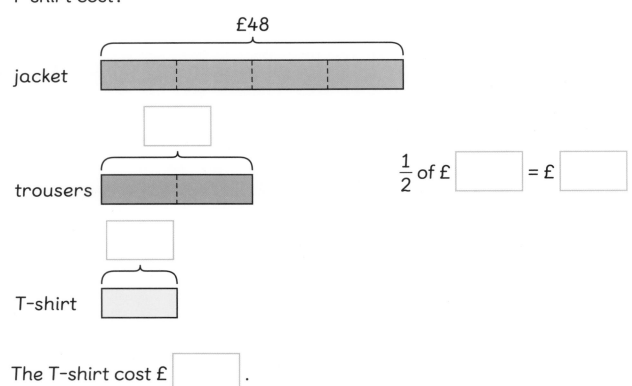

$\frac{1}{2}$ of £ ☐ = £ ☐

The T-shirt cost £ ☐ .

3 Lulu started her homework at 4 o'clock and finished at half past four.
    She took half as long to finish her homework as her older sister did.

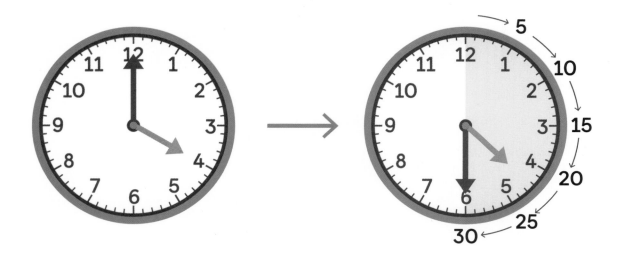

How long did it take Lulu's older sister to do her homework?

Lulu's older sister took ☐ to do her homework.

4 Look at the pictures and fill in the blanks.

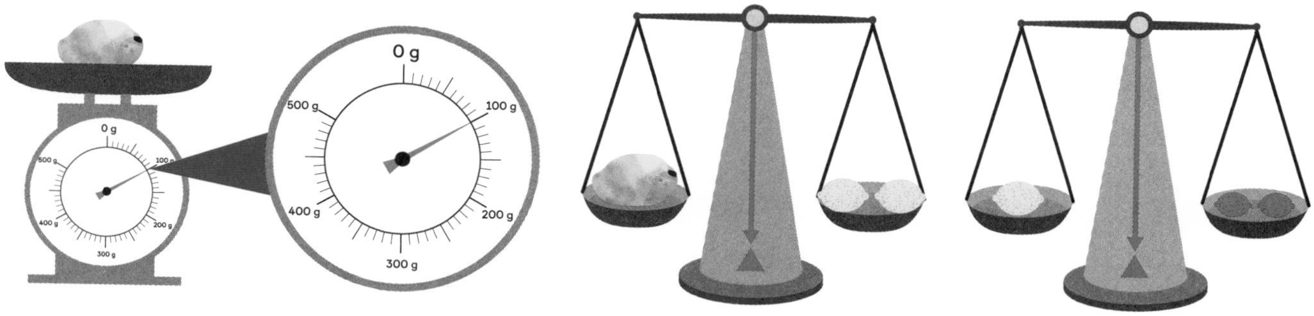

(a) The 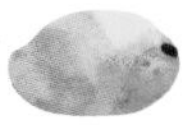 weighs ☐ g.

(b) One  weighs $\frac{☐}{☐}$ as much as one 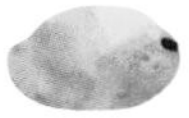.

(c) One  weighs ☐ g.

(d) One  weighs $\frac{☐}{☐}$ as much as one .

(e) One  weighs $\frac{☐}{☐}$ as much as one 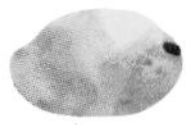.

(f) One  weighs ☐ g.

Review and challenge

1 Circle the shapes that show equal parts.

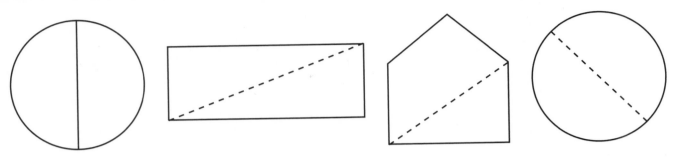

2 Draw lines on each shape to show:

(a) $\frac{1}{2}$

(b) $\frac{1}{4}$

 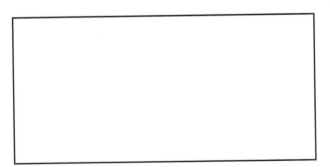

(c) $\frac{1}{3}$

3 What fraction of the shape is shaded?

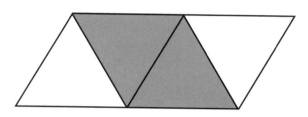

☐ out of ☐ parts is shaded.

☐ is the numerator.

☐ is the denominator.

4 Fill in the blanks.

(a) $\dfrac{2}{\boxed{}} = 1$

(b) $\dfrac{\boxed{}}{3} = 1$

(c) $\dfrac{\boxed{}}{2} = \dfrac{2}{4}$

(d) $\dfrac{2}{4} = \dfrac{1}{\boxed{}}$

(e) $\dfrac{3}{\boxed{}} = 1$

(f) $\dfrac{\boxed{}}{4} = 1$

5 Shade and fill in the blanks.

(a)

| | | | | $\dfrac{3}{4}$

| | | | | $\dfrac{1}{2}$

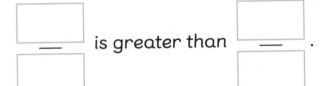

☐/☐ is greater than ☐/☐ .

☐/☐ is smaller than ☐/☐ .

(b)

| | | | $\dfrac{2}{3}$

| | | | | $\dfrac{3}{4}$

☐/☐ is greater than ☐/☐ .

☐/☐ is smaller than ☐/☐ .

6 Fill in the blanks.

(a)

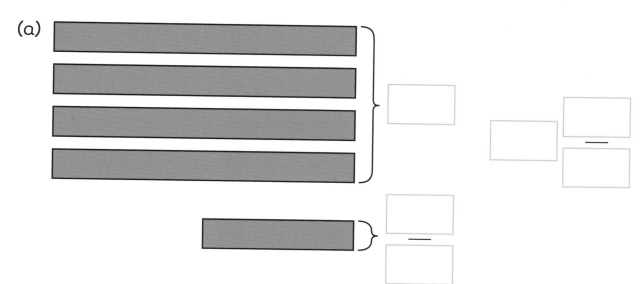

(b)

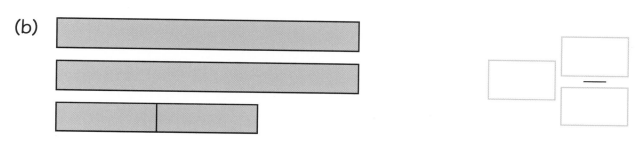

(c)

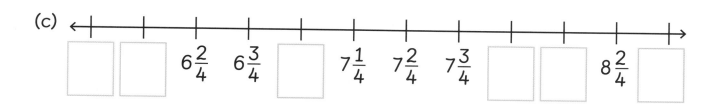

$6\frac{2}{4}$ $6\frac{3}{4}$ $7\frac{1}{4}$ $7\frac{2}{4}$ $7\frac{3}{4}$ $8\frac{2}{4}$

7 Draw an arrow where $8\frac{3}{4}$ is on the number line.

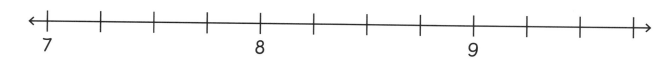

7   8   9

8 Draw an arrow where $5\frac{1}{3}$ is on the number line.

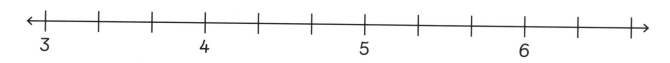

3   4   5   6

9 Fill in the blanks.

(a)

$\frac{1}{3}$ of 27 =

(b)

$\frac{1}{4}$ of 36 =

(c)

$\frac{1}{2}$ of 50 =

10 weighs 20 kg.

Her dog weighs $\frac{1}{2}$ as much as .

Her cat weighs $\frac{1}{4}$ as much as .

How much do the dog and the cat weigh altogether?

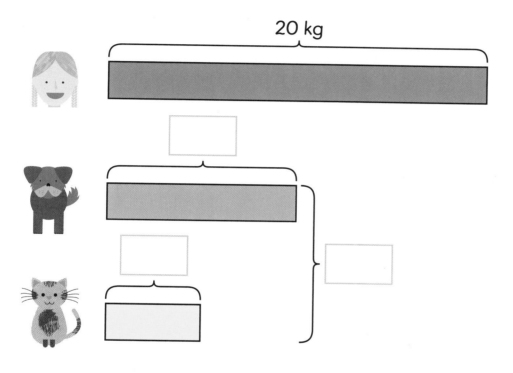

The dog and the cat weigh kg altogether.

Answers

Page 6   **1 (a)** Possible answers:

             (b) Possible answers:

             2 (a) Possible answers:

             (b) Possible answers:

Page 7   **3**

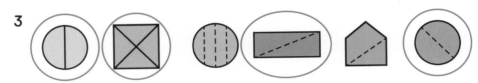

Page 9

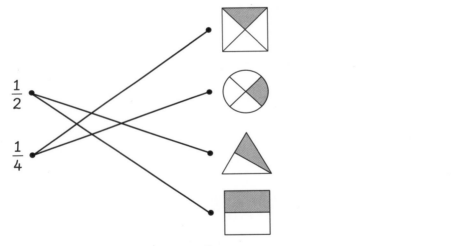

Page 11   **1** $\frac{2}{3}$, 2 thirds   **2** $\frac{1}{3}$, 1 third   **3** $\frac{3}{3}$, 3 thirds

Page 13   **1 (a)** 2 parts out of 4 parts are shaded. 2 is the numerator. 4 is the denominator.
               (b) 1 part out of 4 parts is shaded. 1 is the numerator. 4 is the denominator.
               (c) 1 part out of 2 parts is shaded. 1 is the numerator. 2 is the denominator.   **2** $\frac{2}{4}$, $\frac{2}{4}$

Page 16   **1**

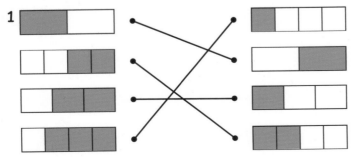

Page 17   **2 (a)** $\frac{2}{2} = 1$ **(b)** $\frac{3}{3} = 1$ **(c)** $\frac{3}{3} = 1$ **(d)** $\frac{4}{4} = 1$ **(e)** $\frac{1}{2} = \frac{2}{4}$ **(f)** $\frac{2}{4} = \frac{1}{2}$

Page 19   **1** Any 1 part shaded, for example:

Any 3 parts shaded, for example: , $\frac{3}{4}$ is greater than $\frac{1}{4}$. $\frac{1}{4}$ is smaller than $\frac{3}{4}$.

2 (a) $\frac{3}{4}, \frac{2}{4}, \frac{1}{4}$ **(b)** $\frac{1}{3}, \frac{2}{3}, \frac{3}{3}$

Page 21   **1 (a)** $\frac{1}{4} < \frac{1}{2}$ **(b)** $\frac{1}{3} > \frac{1}{4}$ **(c)** $\frac{1}{3} < \frac{1}{2}$ **2** $\frac{1}{4}, \frac{1}{3}, \frac{1}{2}$

Page 23   **1** $2, \frac{3}{4}, 2\frac{3}{4}$ **2** $1, \frac{1}{3}, 1\frac{1}{3}$ **3** $2, \frac{1}{2}, 2\frac{1}{2}$ **4** $3, \frac{1}{4}, 3\frac{1}{4}$

Page 25   **1 (a)** $1\frac{1}{2}$ **(b)** $4, \frac{1}{2}, 4\frac{1}{2}$ **(c)** $3\frac{1}{2}$ **2** $2, 3\frac{1}{2}, 4\frac{1}{2}, 5\frac{1}{2}$

Page 27   **1 (a)** $1\frac{1}{4}$ **(b)** $3, \frac{2}{4}, 3\frac{2}{4}$ **(c)** $2\frac{3}{4}$ **2 (a)** $\frac{2}{4}, 1\frac{1}{4}$ **(b)** $7, 7\frac{3}{4}, 8\frac{1}{4}, 8\frac{3}{4}$

Page 29   **1 (a)** $1\frac{1}{3}$ **(b)** $2, \frac{2}{3}, 2\frac{2}{3}$ **(c)** $2\frac{2}{3}$ **2 (a)** $\frac{1}{3}, \frac{2}{3}, 1\frac{2}{3}, 2\frac{2}{3}, 3, 3\frac{1}{3}$ **(b)** $5, 5\frac{1}{3}, 5\frac{2}{3}, 6\frac{2}{3}, 7\frac{2}{3}, 8, 8\frac{1}{3}$

Page 31   **1** 3   **2** 6   **3** 2   **4** 15

Page 33   **1** 4   **2** 5   **3** 4   **4** 12

Page 35

Page 37   **1** 4 m, $\frac{1}{4}$ of 16 m = 4 m. The car is 4 m long.   **2 (a)** £24, $\frac{1}{2}$ of £48 = £24. The trousers cost £24.

Page 38   **(b)** £24 (trousers), $\frac{1}{2}$ of £24 is £12. £12 (T-shirt). The T-shirt cost £12.   **3** Lulu's older sister took 60 minutes OR 1 hour to do her homework.

Page 39   **4 (a)** The mango weighs 100 g.   **(b)** One lemon weighs $\frac{1}{2}$ as much as one mango.

(c) One lemon weighs 50 g.   **(d)** One lime weighs $\frac{1}{2}$ as much as one lemon.

(e) One lime weighs $\frac{1}{4}$ as much as one mango.   **(f)** One lime weighs 25 g.

Answers continued

Page 40 **1** Possible answers:

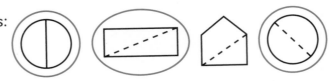

2 (a) Possible answers:

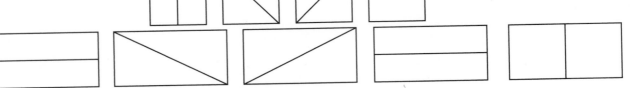

(b) Possible answers:

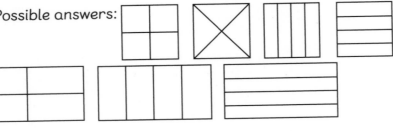

Page 41 **(c)** Possible answers:

3 2 out of 4 parts is shaded. 2 is the numerator. 4 is the denominator.

4 (a) $\frac{2}{2} = 1$ **(b)** $\frac{3}{3} = 1$ **(c)** $\frac{1}{2} = \frac{2}{4}$ **(d)** $\frac{2}{4} = \frac{1}{2}$ **(e)** $\frac{3}{3} = 1$ **(f)** $\frac{4}{4} = 1$

Page 42 **5 (a)** Any 3 parts shaded, for example:

Any 2 parts shaded, for example:

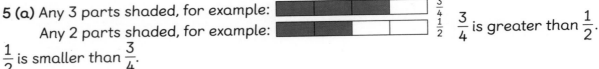

$\frac{3}{4}$ is greater than $\frac{1}{2}$.

$\frac{1}{2}$ is smaller than $\frac{3}{4}$.

(b) Any 2 parts shaded, for example:

Any 3 parts shaded, for example:

$\frac{3}{4}$ is greater than $\frac{2}{3}$.

$\frac{2}{3}$ is smaller than $\frac{3}{4}$.

Page 43 **6 (a)** 4, $\frac{1}{2}$, 4$\frac{1}{2}$ **(b)** 2$\frac{2}{3}$ **(c)** 6, 6$\frac{1}{4}$, 7, 8, 8$\frac{1}{4}$, 8$\frac{3}{4}$

7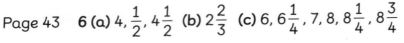

8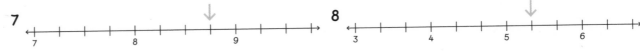

Page 44 **9 (a)** 9 **(b)** 9 **(c)** 25

Page 45 **10** 10 kg (dog), 5 kg (cat), 15 kg. The dog and cat weigh 15 kg altogether.